BEFORE

ELVIS

there was nothing

BEFORE
ELVIS
there was nothing

PATRICK HIGGINS

CARROLL & GRAF PUBLISHERS
NEW YORK

Copyright © 1994
by Patrick T. Higgins

First Carroll & Graf edition 1994

Carroll & Graf Publishers, Inc.
260 Fifth Avenue
New York, NY 10001

Library of Congress Cataloging-in-Publication Data

Before Elvis, there was nothing / edited by Patrick Higgins.
  — 1st Carroll & Graf ed.
     p. cm.
  ISBN 0-7867-0145-5 : $11.95
    1. Presley, Elvis, 1935–1977—Quotations. 2. Presley,
Elvis 1935–1977—Portraits. I. Higgins, Patrick, 1962–
ML420.P96B46 1994
782.42166′092—dc20   94-3475
                                          CIP
                                          MN

Book design by Studio 31

Acknowledgments

There are two people in particular that I want to thank.

First my mother Kathleen for not throwing out her Elvis records in 1958 and more importantly for her love and support. And my best friend Mary Cameron Bitel, without whose constant encouragement, hand holding, support and love, this book would never have happened.

I would also like to thank my agent Philip Spitzer, who while not an Elvis fan (though we're working on that) believed in the project and took it on. Also to Kent Carroll, Jennifer Prior and everyone at Carroll & Graf for their wonderful job in making this book a reality, and to Jim Wasserman for his great design.

Thanks also to Anne-Lise Spitzer, Jeff Frankel and Tim Tobias.

And of course most of all to "The King." We'll never see his like again.

Author's Note

On a January night in 1956, while Perry Como sang his latest hit, "Hot Diggedy, Dog Diggedy" on NBC's "Your Hit Parade" a young truck driver from Memphis, Tennessee was appearing on CBS.

He was unlike any entertainer America had seen before. From the moment he walked on stage people knew something was at risk. The music he chose was alarming — black rhythm and blues born out of the pain and sorrow of the Mississippi Delta. Songs which contained lyrics most Americans at the time found inappropriate for even the seediest dance halls, much less national TV. Witness *Shake, Rattle and Roll* where he proclaimed "I'm like a one-eyed cat, peepin' in a seafood store. I can look at you until you ain't no child no more."

Even his name was dangerous — Elvis Presley.

Not only did he sound dangerous, he looked it. Jet black hair combed back into a perfect DA; black rayon suit with the collar turned up; a sneer turning up his lip, and a smoldering stare.

He was Evil personified deposited into America's living room. And around the country, people watched in rapt awe —especially the women, young women. This wasn't the guy you waited for by the phone to ask you down to "Pop's Soda Shop" for a root beer float — this was someone you wanted to get sweaty with in the back seat of a '56 Chevy. This was the bad stuff. The good bad stuff.

One of those young women was my mother. For her and her friends from St. Joseph's High School, Elvis's first appearance on television was an event. She and her friends organized a pot luck dinner at one of their homes to watch. As my grandparents sent her off with her contribution of a jello mold, they had no idea what the hoopla was about. Why the commotion? They watched "The Dorsey Brothers Variety Hour" every week and never failed to be entertained by an evening that might include a 25-member xylophone band and a one-armed juggler. Good, clean, wholesome entertainment.

That's what the Dorseys were. Little did they know they were sending their only daughter off to be hit in the head with an atomic bomb.

When my mother returned home my grandfather was livid. "Did you watch that disgusting singer tonight Kathleen?"

"Yes," she replied.

"That's it!" he boomed, "First thing tomorrow, you're going to confession!"

The next morning, confessionals in Catholic churches around the country were filled to overflowing with guilt ridden young girls wearing shit-eating grins wide across their faces. It was liberation and they loved it — but they were also ashamed.

As for the men, this was the guy they had always wanted to be. The one who could drive girls into a frenzy with just a stare. The one who could move with the energy and passion they had always felt inside but couldn't bring to the surface. He was simply, "The Baddest Cat on the Planet."

For most Elvis fans, like me, this is the Elvis we remember and always will. It's the memory of this Elvis, "The Hillbilly Cat," that enabled him years later, when he had become a pathetic, obese caricature of his former self, to still command the sellout audiences of screaming fans. It's why thousands of people each year make a pilgrimage to Memphis to visit Graceland. And it's the memory of this Elvis that sent millions of people to the U.S. Post Office on the anniversary of his birthday in 1993 to buy a stamp bearing his image. He is the ultimate symbol of youth in all its intoxication.

But this is only how I see it — someone who's been an Elvis fan since he uncovered his mother's 45 rpm of *Hound Dog* and *Don't Be Cruel* in a box in his grandparents'attic. I wondered — did *everyone* play that same 45 over and over until the grooves were worn flat?

How do other people see Elvis? With love or disdain? As a hero or a clown? As the "King of Rock and Roll" or simply a hillbilly who was in the right place at the right time?

That's what this book is about. It is in its way a biography, but makes no final judgement, reaches no conclusion. It is impossible to do so, for both the man and the myth are far too complex. It is simply a story told by a few people who glimpsed Elvis as he passed through their lives. Some who knew him and some who were just looking from the outside in at the most recognizable cultural icon America has ever produced.

— Patrick Higgins
New York City
June 1994

*B*efore Elvis, there was nothing.

— JOHN LENNON

$\mathcal{T}$he image is one thing
and the human being is another . . .
it's very hard to live up to an image.

— Elvis Presley

*G*ladys holds her precious son
to her side. She has two men in her life
now who will depend on her and she on
them, and as she looks into the eyes of her
devoted husband, she whispers the name
of their beloved son that God has chosen
for them — Elvis Aron Presley.

— VESTER PRESLEY
Elvis's uncle on Elvis's
birth

*E*lvis's neighbors were the people who drove trucks and worked in gas stations and spent their youth in roadside taverns listening to tales of their heartbreak hotel. Their life was an Elvis song.

— Robert Carey
*The Memphis
Commercial Appeal*

*E*lvis came out for the boxing team at Humes High School. I put him in the ring against Sambo Barrom and this guy bloodied Elvis's nose pretty good. Then Elvis came to me and said, "Coach, I hate to tell you this, but I'm quitting the team. I'm a lover, not a fighter."

— WALT DOXEY
Elvis's high school
boxing coach

RULEMAN, SHIRLEY

Major: Home Ec., Commercial, English.
Activities: National Honor Society, F. H. A., Y-Teens, Latin Club, Cheerleader, Sabre Club, History Club, English Club, Honorary Capta in R. O. T. C., President Home Ec. Class.

PRESLEY, ELVIS ARON

Major: Shop, History, English.
Activities: R. O. T. C., Biology Club, English Club, History Club, Spee Club.

PERRY, ROBERT EARL

Major: History, Science, English.
Activities: Biology Club, T&I Club, Key Club, Baseball 4 years, Vic President Key Club, Boys' Vice-President Senior Class, President T&I Clu
Awards: All-Star American Legion Baseball Team 1952, National Hon Society.

SANDERS, MARY LOUISE

Major: Commercial, Band, English.
Activities: Senior Band, Y-Teens, English Club, History Club, Historia of Band.

He used to come around and
be around us a lot. There was a place we
used to go and hang out at on Beale Street.
We used to just hang out and play. That
was the first place I met him.

— B. B. KING

If I could find a white man who had
the Negro sound and the Negro feel,
I could make a million dollars.

— SAM PHILLIPS

*H*e sings nigger music.

— An RCA
record executive

*L*ike a young boxer
after his first professional knockout,
Presley is dizzy with the confirmation of
his prowess. "Blue Moon of Kentucky" is
daring to the point of mania. It is Elvis
walking on steel blades, through
orange-white flames, invincible with the
knowledge he sees in Sam's eyes, hears in
his own voice, and feels in his own flushed
skin; the knowledge that right now,
this moment, he, Elvis Aron Presley,
is the greatest singer in Memphis
and the universe.

— NICK TOSCHES
Rock critic

He was ahead of his time
because he had deep feelings. He had
the privilege of deep feelings because he
was deeply loved by his mother, Gladys.
He was able to appreciate deep, profound
beauty in sounds. And he started a
musical revolution. They say all
revolutions start from love.

— IMELDA MARCOS

I saw Elvis live in '54. It was at
the Big D Jamboree in Dallas and the first
thing, he came out and spit on the stage . . .
it affected me exactly the same way as
when I first saw that David Lynch film.
There was just no reference point in
the culture to compare it.

— ROY ORBISON

*T*his cat come out in red pants
and a green coat and a pink shirt and
socks and he had this sneer on his face
and he stood behind the mike for five
minutes, I'll bet, before he made a move.
Then he hit his guitar a lick, and broke two
strings. So there he was, these two strings
dangling, and he hadn't done anything
yet, and these high school girls were
screaming and fainting and running up
to the stage, and then he started to
move his hips real slow like he
had a thing for his guitar.

— BOB LUMEN
Country singer

*H*e's just one big hunk of forbidden fruit.

— A young female fan on
why Elvis made her
flip

I promise
that I shall not take part
in the reception accorded
Elvis Presley
and I shall not be present
at the program presented by him
at the Auditorium
on Wednesday,
April 3, 1957.

— OATH
signed by students of the
Notre Dame Convent
School, Ottawa, Canada

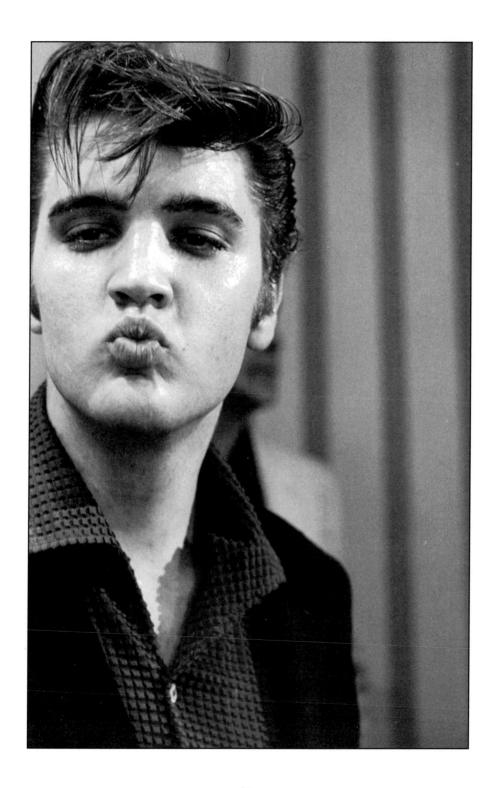

*T*wo guys hanging from
the balcony railing dropped down
into the mob, apparently to get closer
to Elvis. One girl kicked an usher in the
stomach and they carried him out with the
others, who had apparently fainted.

— ARLENE COGAN
Journalist

When I first heard Elvis's voice
I just knew that I wasn't going to work
for anybody; and nobody was going to be
my boss. He is the deity supreme of rock
& roll religion as it exists in today's form.
Hearing him for the first time was
like busting out of jail.

— BOB DYLAN

*P*resley defined rock and roll in 1956.
The sneer. The hair. The twisting knees.
The thrusting hips. The pink Cadillac.

— DICK CLARK

I believe the three most important events
of the 1950s were the Brown vs. the Board
of Education decision, the building of
Levittown, and the emergence
of Elvis Presley.

— DAVID HALBERSTAM

*W*hen we were kids,
growing up in Liverpool, all we ever
wanted to be was Elvis Presley.

— PAUL McCARTNEY

$\mathcal{H}$e's a great singer. Gosh, he's so great.
You have no idea how great he is, really,
you don't. You have absolutely no
comprehension — it's absolutely
impossible. I can't tell you why
he's so great, but he is.

— PHIL SPECTOR

*H*e had a keen ear.
He wasn't a fantastic musician,
but he played just enough to know
what he was talking about. And when he
heard what he wanted to hear, he'd say,
"That's it, man, don't change nothin'."

— D. J. FONTANA
Elvis's drummer

I set the session for the afternoon,
and he came in with pink trousers with
blue stripes and he was real nice. . . . He
was singing and split his pants. One of the
boys went out to get him another pair and
he threw the split pair in the corner.
A girl who was working for the
Methodist Publishing Company in
the same building asked what to do with
the pants, and I told her she better hang on
to them, that boy's gonna be famous.
She said, "Naw." Six months later
there she was on *I've Got a Secret*
with Elvis's pants.

— CHET ATKINS

Elvis Presley was more than anything
a spiritual leader of our generation —
there is really no way to assess his
importance, much less the meaning
of the music he created.

— Dave Marsh

$\mathcal{H}$e can't last. I tell you flatly, he can't last.

— JACKIE GLEASON

I wouldn't have Presley
on my show at any time.

— ED SULLIVAN

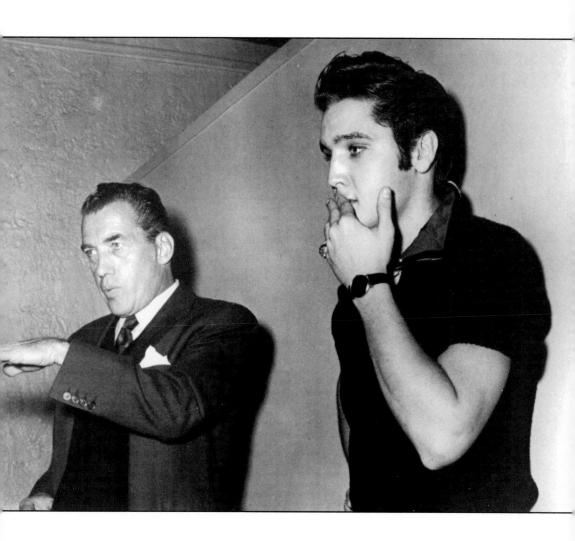

After his famous first appearance on
The Ed Sullivan Show in 1956, my aunt told
me how foolish I was to sit screaming with
joy at the spectacle of that vulgar singer on
TV. It was then I knew that she and I lived
in different worlds, and it was then that
kids' bedroom doors slammed
all over America.

— MAUREEN ORTH
Newsweek

*I*t isn't enough to say
that Elvis is kind to his parents, sends
money home, and is the same unspoiled
kid he was before all the commotion began.
That still isn't a free ticket to behave
like a sex maniac in public.

— EDDIE CONDON
Cosmopolitan

*E*lvis Presley is the greatest cultural force
in the 20th century. He introduced the beat
to everything and he changed everything
— music, language, clothes, it's a whole
new social revolution. Because of him
a man like me barely knows his
musical grammar anymore.

— LEONARD BERNSTEIN

*H*is kind of music is deplorable,
a rancid-smelling aphrodisiac.

— FRANK SINATRA

*E*lvis died when he went into the army.

— JOHN LENNON

I'd rather try and
close a deal with the devil.

— HAL WALLIS
Director
on Colonel Tom Parker

*T*he really thought-provoking
thing about this movie isn't the plot
though, but Elvis. I think in this movie,
Elvis demonstrates once and for all
how downright unfair it is to call him a
teenage menace. Nobody in the audience
yowled or shrieked or moaned or went
out of their mind or anything.
Everybody just sat there.
That's because they realize
Elvis is a real actor, and I think
that when Marilyn Monroe does
The Brothers Karamazov, like she said
she would, Elvis ought to be in it too.
He'd be just great as the other brother.

— *The New Republic*
From a tongue-in-cheek
review of *Love Me Tender*
December 1956

I love the Elvis movies.
I used to watch them. In every
single one of his movies he wasn't acting
as a car salesman — he was acting as a car
salesman who loved to play guitar.

— LARRY MULLEN
U2 drummer

On the set of *Girls! Girls! Girls!*
he was drunk part of the time and
showing me his pill book the other part
of the time. I was not interested in pills.
He was so insecure when he sang
"Return to Sender" — with an audience
full of extras paid to applaud him — that he
would get totally drunk before he went on.

— STELLA STEVENS

*T*alkin' about eatin' pussy,
me and Sam Phillips used to make old Elvis
sick with that stuff. We'd sit around the
studio, down at Sun Records, and talk
about how good it was, and he'd get so
sick he'd go out back and puke.
Then he went to Hollywood, made all
them movies and came back, and one night
we're all down at the studio, Elvis and Sam
and me, and Jerry Lee Lewis, whole bunch
of us there, and Elvis says, "Mister Sam,
you remember when ya'll used to make me
sick talkin' about eatin' pussy?"
Sam says, "What about it?"
"Well," Elvis says, "I eat me some the
other night. But man, now I'm in trouble."
So Sam asks him, "Who was it you eat?"
because we thought right off that Elvis
had eat somebody's wife and got caught.
But he says, "Natalie Wood," and Sam
says, "Well, hell-fire boy, what's your
trouble?" and Elvis said, "Damn if
I didn't fall in love with it."

— DEWEY PHILLIPS

*A*fter we finished shooting
some days we would hear that
there was a party at Elvis's house.
We'd go up there but it wasn't really
much of a party at all. It was just a
bunch of girls sitting around Elvis,
watching him watch TV.

— TERI GARR

*I*t was the finest music of his life.
If there was ever music that bleeds, this
was it. Nothing came easy that night
and he gave everything he had —
more than anyone knew he had.

— Greil Marcus
on the
'68 comeback special

*T*hat's my idol, Elvis Presley.
If you went to my house, you'd see
pictures all over of Elvis.
He's just the greatest entertainer
that ever lived. And I think it's because
he had so much presence. When Elvis
Presley walked into a room, Elvis Presley
was in the fucking room. I don't give a fuck
who was in the room with him, Bogart,
Marilyn Monroe.

— EDDIE MURPHY

*H*e taught me everything;
how to dress, how to walk, how to
apply makeup and wear my hair, how to
return love — his way. Over the years
he became my father, husband,
and very nearly God.

— Priscilla Presley

At 9:15 Elvis appeared,
materialized, in a white suit of lights,
shining with golden appliqués,
the shirtfront slashed to show his chest.
Around his shoulders was a cape lined in
a cloth of gold, its collar faced with scarlet.
It was anything you wanted to call it,
gaudy, vulgar — magnificent.

— DONNA MUIR
The New York Times

I sensed that
basically he was a very shy man.
Flamboyance was covering up the shyness.
He wanted to be an example to young
people. And people say that
because later on, it was found that
he had used drugs, that, therefore, he
could not be a good example.
They overlooked the fact
that he never used illegal drugs.
It was always drugs
prescribed by his physician.
But I think he was a very decent man.

— RICHARD NIXON

𝒯oward the end, he was paranoid. He kept in his Bible the police report of two guys who tried to rush him on the stage in 1973. My purse was always searched for weapons before I could go into his suite, and once when the cork of a champagne bottle was popped he ducked for cover and his bodyguards completely surrounded me.

— MICKEY
a secretary at a
Las Vegas hotel

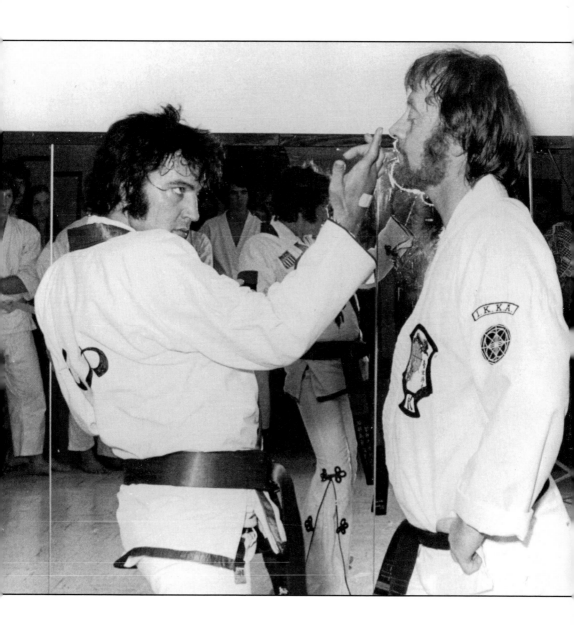

*T*he last time he sang in Las Vegas
he telephoned and said,
"You haven't been over, chief,"
so I said OK and went to see his show.
But I didn't want to go
because I loved my friend and
didn't want to see his decline. . . .
It was obvious to me that this was Elvis's
swan song because practically every song
he sang was a way of saying good-bye:
"My Way," "Take My Hand Precious
Lord," "Just A Closer Walk With Thee."
He must have done nine of these songs.
He was saying good-bye to the world.
Anyone who was tuned in
had to realize that he had had it.

— WAYNE NEWTON

The King is dead.

— *Tupelo Daily Journal*
Headline
August 17, 1977

*W*e've lost
the most popular man
that ever walked on this planet
since Christ himself was here.

— CARL PERKINS

$\mathcal{M}$y partner and I
had been called to a real tough
neighborhood because of a domestic
dispute. When we got there, this couple
was just about to kill each other.
The woman had the man
down and was choking him.
We pulled them apart.
Just then, it came over our radio
that Elvis had died. The woman started
crying and the man went limp.
This seemed to take their attention
from their fight and they went to watching
TV and talking about Elvis. We didn't hear
anything more from them that night.

— CURT WALLIS
Shelby County
deputy sheriff

*E*lvis in his coffin was fat, glowering, and surrounded by similar-looking but vertical heavies who pushed us viewers along. Reportedly Elvis had died "straining at the stool" while reading a book about the discovery of Christ's remains. ELVIS DEAD, alright. But not at peace. He looked like he wanted to make another big leap, but couldn't. He didn't look cool.

— Roy Blount, Jr.

As Jennifer was dying,
she seemed to light up. The light
looked as though it were coming from
within her. She smiled a big smile. Jimmy
and I were hugging her and crying and
she tried to sit up. She said,
"I love you Mommy and Daddy."
Then she said, "Here comes Elvis."
She was looking upwards and holding
her arms out like she was trying to reach
toward someone and hug them. She said
it twice, "Here comes Elvis." Then
she collapsed and died.

— SHERRY REED
on the death of her
11-year-old daughter

*W*hen he awoke at 3:00 P.M.,
Elvis would take a vitamin "voice shot,"
medication for dizziness, a laxative, three
uppers and testosterone. An hour before
the show, he'd have another voice shot,
plus drugs for vertigo, a decongestant with
codeine, an upper and Dilaudid. At show
time, he'd add diluted caffeine, Dexedrine
and more Dilaudid. After the show
he'd take a blood-pressure pill, an
antihistamine, a tranquilizer, a sedative
and diluted Demerol. At bedtime there
were Quaaludes or Placidyl, plus an
upper, a laxative, a blood pressure
pill and three more sedatives.

— DR. GEORGE
NICHOPOULOS
Elvis's doctor
From the trial testimony

Presley's Doctor Acquitted On All Prescription Charges

Special to The New York Times

MEMPHIS, Nov. 4 — Dr. George Nichopoulos was acquitted today of 11 counts of criminally overprescribing addictive drugs to Elvis Presley, the country-western singer Jerry Lee Lewis and seven other patients.

The jury of six men and six women deliberated just over three hours before reaching the unanimous verdict for the acquittal on all counts.

Dr. Nichopoulos, 54 years old, hugged his wife, Edna, after the verdict was returned and shook hands with friends and other family members, including his two daughters, Elaine and Chrissie, who had crowded into the Memphis courtroom.

"I'm truly happy for Dr. Nichopoulos," the defense attorney, James F. Neal, said. "I think he's been harassed for years. He is very thankful."

Two of the jurors later congratulated Mr. Neal on his handling of the case.

Directed Acquittal on 3 Counts

Judge Bernie Weinman of Criminal Court had directed acquittal of three counts against Dr. Nichopolous last week. The decision came after a witness for the prosecution had testified that there could have been a valid medical justification for the drugs the doctor was charged with prescribing for himself and a patient, Robert Deason.

In final arguments before the jury retired, Dr. Nichopoulos, who was indicted last January, was alternately portrayed as a kind-hearted samaritan and as a physician with almost total disregard for accepted standards of medical practice.

Mr. Neal argued in his closing statement that Dr. Nichopoulos was a "good samaritan" who treated drug-depend-

Associated Press

Dr. George Nichopoulos yesterday in Memphis after the verdict.

ent patients whom no other doctor wanted to accept.

"I can't think of anything that fits Dr. Nichopoulos better," Mr. Neal told the jury, referring to the biblical parable. "Dr. George Nichopoulos is the man — the man who stopped and looked at these people and then offered to help. You are judging the samaritan."

Prosecutors' View

However, the prosecutors, Jim Wilson and Jewett Miller, had another interpretation of Dr. Nichopoulos's actions. He was, they said, a physician who abused his authority in dispensing dangerous and addictive drugs.

In three weeks of testimony, the prosecutors showed that Dr. Nichopoulos prescribed more than 19,000 doses of narcotics, sedatives and stimulants to Mr. Presley in the 31½ months before the entertainer died Aug. 16, 1977.

They also showed that he prescribed a variety of stimulants and sedatives to Mr. Lewis and the other patients.

Dr. Nichopoulos acknowledged from the witness stand that he had prescribed the drugs, but he said many of those prescribed for Mr. Presley were thrown away or substituted with placebos, harmless, inert substances.

Patients Already Had Problem

He also said all nine patients mentioned in the 11-count indictment had been getting drugs from other sources and already had a drug problem when they first came to him for treatment. Dr. Nichopolous said he gave them drugs in the hope of eliminating the other drug sources and then, once he became their sole supplier, weaning them from their drug dependency.

The prosecutors, who called 13 witnesses to the stand, were unable to establish clearly any other motive for the prescriptions.

Dr. Nichopoulos received loans totaling $280,000 from Mr. Presley, but they were properly signed and executed and are being repaid, according to Beecher Smith, the attorney for the entertainer's estate.

Dr. Nichopoulos made little money from the other patients mentioned in the indictment, testimony showed. Mr. Lewis, for instance, paid an average of $9.10 for each examination he received from Dr. Nichopoulos.

Nonetheless, Dr. Alvin Cummins, a Memphis internist, testified that he could find no legitimate medical reason for any of the patients to receive the drugs. Such prescriptions, he said, were clearly contrary to accepted standards of medical practice.

However, Dr. Forest Tennant Jr., a drug researcher at the University of California at Los Angeles and one of 14 defense witnesses, said Dr. Nichopoulos might have made the wisest possible medical choice in prescribing the drugs while attempting to control the patients' intake.

I was at the checkout,
picking up my groceries. I looked up
and there he was, Elvis. I couldn't believe
it. I was speechless, I mean you're not
expecting to run into Elvis Presley
in the grocery store.

— LOUISE WELLING,
    a Kalamazoo housewife,
    on her sighting of
    Elvis in 1987

SOLVE AMERICA'S BIGGEST CROSSWORD PUZZLE — AND WIN $2,500 IN PRIZES!

WEEKLY WORLD NEWS

September 6, 1994   99¢/$1.09 CANADA   70p UK

59-yr.-old King speaks for the first time since his fake funeral in 1977!

ELVIS TELLS LISA MARIE: DIVORCE MICHAEL!

WORLD EXCLUSIVE! *Read the blistering letter he wrote to his daughter!*

*E*lvis,

You died so young and beautiful
15 years ago today. I watched in silence
as they carried you away. As I stand here
today I just can't stop thinkin' 'bout you.
You're always on my mind.

Loving you,
Renee

— Message inscribed
on the wall around
Graceland

I remember standin' in front
of those gates with guitar players on 'em
and looking up toward the house. . . .
So I jumped over the wall and started
running toward the front door . . . .
I got to the front door, and guards came
out of the bushes and they asked me what
I wanted. And I said, "Is Elvis home?"
And they said, "No, he's in Lake Tahoe."
So I tried to tell them that I was a
guitar player and had my own band, and
that we had played in town that night, and
that Elvis was my inspiration. They took
me by the arm and put me back out on
the street. . . . It wasn't long after that
when a friend called and told me that he
died. And I started thinking about what I
would have done if Elvis had come to the
door. And I realized it wasn't really Elvis I
was going to see at all, but some dream I
had of him. It's like he came along and
whispered a dream in everybody's ear,
and then we all dreamed it somehow.

— BRUCE SPRINGSTEEN

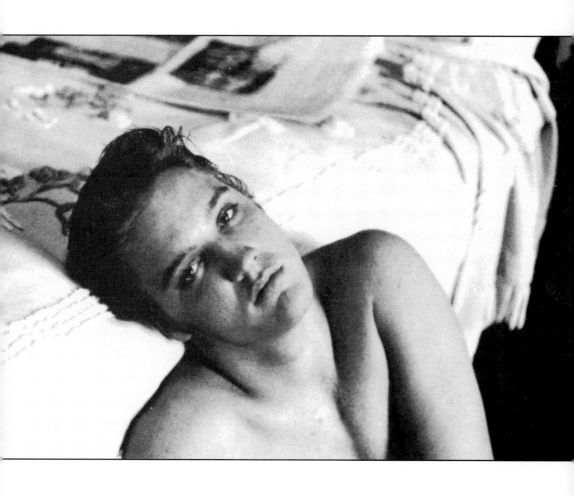

He is loved, he is hated.
He was a genius, a fraud. A saint,
the devil. The King, the clown.
Even more than when he was alive,
Elvis has come to symbolize everything
great and everything hideous about
America. And all the poor guy wanted
to do was buy a few Cadillacs, sing his
songs and make a decent movie
somewhere along the line.

— BILL HOLDSHIP
BAM Magazine

*T*he question
of Elvis Presley
remains as alive as
the man himself is dead.
He remains the specter of possibility —
in rock and roll, pop culture,
"America," modern life —
and he remains the fact of ruin.
Solve the question if you can,
say the specter and the fact — or else
drop the question of who you are,
where you came from, and
where you might end up.

— GREIL MARCUS

Credits

$\mathcal{T}$he quotes that appear here were culled from a variety of sources; newspapers, magazines, reprinted excerpts of articles and books as well as radio and television interviews.

PAGE 13   *Roger Marshantz*

Elvis performing at the Mississippi State Fair, September 26, 1956 in a navy-blue velvet shirt made by his mother Gladys.

This concert marked Elvis's triumphant return home. Governor J. P. Coleman declared the day "Elvis Presley Day" in the state of Mississippi. When the Governor arrived at the fair that afternoon to present Elvis with the official proclamation, his car was mobbed by a group of shrieking young woman who thought he was Elvis.

Eleven years earlier, Elvis had taken a second place prize at this same fair for his rendition of "Old Shep." This time however, the scene was much different. Not confined by the censors of television, Elvis put on a trademark "Elvis" show. Thousand of girls shrieked, hundreds broke down in hysterics and dozens more fainted. The pandemonium hit its apex as women up front tore the footlights on the stage from their very sockets as photographers were forced to flee across the stage to find refuge. Elvis eventually had to stop the show until the Mississippi National Guard could restore order. Photographer Roger Marshantz was on one of his first assignments for *Photoplay* magazine when he took the shot. It is the only photo from this assignment that remains. And considering the conditions that in itself is a small miracle.

PAGE 15   *Alfred Wertheimer*

Elvis with an unnamed woman in the stairwell backstage in Richmond, VA., July 22, 1956.

In 1956, photographer Alfred Wertheimer was photographing the musical stars of the time. In March of 1956, Wertheimer photographed Elvis for the first time. From the moment he saw him, Wertheimer knew something special was happening.

Wertheimer recalled photographing Paul Anka, who was crooning his current hit, "Put Your Head on My Shoulder." When Anka would perform his big hit, he would bring a young woman up on stage, put her head on his shoulder, and sing. Maybe every sixth concert, the woman would cry. Not so with Elvis. When he came on stage he would simply stand there, not doing much of anything. The girls still went wild. Screaming, fainting, and yes, crying. "I stayed with Elvis," Wertheimer said, "because he could make the girls cry."

Alfred Wertheimer would stay with Elvis until October of 1956. His photographs remain the most famous and powerful images of the young Elvis Presley and a young rock and roll.

Three of his images appear here.

PAGE 17 *Photographer unknown*

Elvis with his father Vernon and his mother Gladys at the age of three. This is the earliest known photo of Elvis Presley.

PAGE 19 *Globe Photos*

Elvis and an unnamed friend during the Memphis Jaycee car rodeo in the early 1950s.

Here Elvis and his friend measure the distance between the wheel and the curb after a parking test.

PAGE 21 *Photographer unknown*

Elvis in his senior year yearbook photo from Humes High School.

PAGE 23 *Ernest C. Withers*

Elvis and B. B. King backstage at the Memphis City Auditorium, 1956.

PAGE 25 *RCA Records*

Elvis in his first publicity shot issued by RCA Records.

PAGE 27 *Michael Ochs Archives*

PAGE 29 *Michael Ochs Archives*

Elvis performing at the old Florida Theater in 1957.

This photo won the National Press Photographers Association contest in 1957.

PAGE 31 *Alfred Wertheimer*

Elvis and his mother Gladys, July 4, 1956. Elvis's mother gives him a clean pair of underwear before his homecoming concert that evening at Memphis's Russwood Stadium.

PAGE 33 *Photographer unknown*

PAGE 35 *Globe Photos/Rob East*

PAGE 37 *AP/Wide World Photos*

An enthusiastic young female fan reacts at a concert in Philadelphia, PA, April 6, 1957.

PAGE 39 *Globe Photos/Lloyd Dickens*

PAGE 41 *Globe Photos*

PAGE 43 *Michael Ochs Archives*

PAGE 45 *Cinema Collectors*

PAGE 47 *Cinema Collectors*

PAGE 49 *Cinema Collectors*

PAGE 51 *Michael Ochs Archives*

The other guests that evening were Sammy Davis, Jr., Joey Bishop, Peter Lawford and Presley's future co-star, Nancy Sinatra. For many, this was the beginning of the end for Elvis.

PAGE 71 *Blackstar /Charles Bonnay*
Elvis en route to Germany following his induction in 1958.

PAGE 73 *Photographer unknown*

PAGE 75 *Cinema Collectors*
Elvis in his dramatic death scene from "Love Me Tender," with co-stars Richard Egan and Deborah Paget. This scene horrified many Presley fans, as they simply couldn't bear the thought of Elvis dying.

PAGE 77 *Cinema Collectors*
Elvis and co-star Joan Blackman in a scene from "Blue Hawaii."

PAGE 79 *Michael Ochs Archives*
Elvis and Stella Stevens on the set of "Girls, Girls, Girls."

PAGE 81 *Michael Ochs Archives*
Elvis and Natalie Wood.

PAGE 83 *Michael Ochs Archives*
Elvis in scene from "Roustabout." On his left is a young and as of yet unknown, Terri Garr. Earlier, Garr had appeared in another Presley movie, "Viva Las Vegas."

PAGE 85 *Michael Ochs Archives*
Elvis during a number from his 1968 comeback special.
When originally scheduled, Col. Parker intended the show to be "A Christmas Card from Elvis and the Colonel," with Presley packing as many Christmas carols as possible into one hour, the whole time surrounded by various dancing Santas and elves.
Elvis and Producer/Director Steve Binder had other ideas. Elvis had grown tired of the movie image he had been saddled with after 31 formula films. He wanted to show everyone that he could still rock the house. Unfortunately, Elvis was still unable to break free from the Colonel and his questionable advise. Binder came up with an idea. He told Elvis that the two of them would take a stroll down Sunset Blvd. If so much as one person noticed and approached Elvis, they would do it the Colonel's way. If no one noticed, they would do it Binder's way. Not a single person recognized Elvis, or if they did, they didn't care. The show was done Binder's way.
The highlight of the show was a sort of backporch, hillbilly jam session with Elvis and members of his original group Scotty Moore and D. J. Fontana performing songs like "Trying to Get to You," and the Jimmy Reed classic, "Baby what Do You Want Me to Do." It was Elvis doing what he did best — sing rock and roll.
Rock critic Jon Landau described the evening like this:
"There is something special about watching a man who has lost

himself find his way back home. He sang with the kind of power people no longer associate with rock and roll singers. He moved his body with the lack of pretension and effort that must have made Jim Morrison green with envy. And while most of the songs were ten or twelve years old, he sang them as freshly as though they were written yesterday."

It was Elvis's last great moment.

PAGE 87   *RCA Records*
Elvis and Sammy Davis, Jr. backstage in Las Vegas.

PAGE 89   *Michael Ochs Archives*

PAGE 91   *Michael Ochs Archives*

PAGE 93   *Michael Ochs Archives*
Elvis and Richard Nixon in the Oval Office, December 21, 1970.

In 1970, Elvis hand wrote a letter on American Airlines stationery to President Nixon. The letter began, "Dear Mr. President, First I would like to introduce myself. I am Elvis Presley and I admire you and I have great respect for your office." Elvis would go on in the letter to voice his support for the President, speak out against the "drug culture and hippie element" in this country, offer his support in any way possible, and request an official DEA badge.

At the time, Richard Nixon realized he was growing increasingly out of touch with the youth of America. Nixon felt it was important to speak with some of the outstanding "young people" in the country. After reading Elvis's letter, Nixon's aids felt that Presley might not be a bad person to start with.

It was arranged that Elvis would meet with Nixon during the open hour held every day to meet with various "regular Americans." Presley arrived with Memphis mafia members, Jerry Shilling and Sonny West. The meeting lasted about twenty minutes with Nixon's most memorable line being, "Boy, you sure dress kind of wild." Elvis left with his special agent DEA badge in hand. To this day it is still a question whether the appointment of "special agent" was real or honorary. Another rumor that exists from this historic meeting is the condition of Elvis himself. Rumor has it that while Elvis stood in the oval office, speaking with the President and receiving of all things a DEA badge, he was so stoned he barely knew where he was.

PAGE 95   *Globe Photos*
Elvis and Memphis mafia member Red West practice karate. For whatever reason, Elvis had grown exceedingly worried about threats to his life in the mid and late seventies. In addition to becoming a black belt in karate, he also sported an impressive collection of hand guns.

PAGE 97   *AP/Wide World Photos*
Elvis performing in Providence, Rhode Island, May 6, 1977.

PAGE 99   *Archive Photos*
A mourner learns of Elvis's death.

PAGE 101   *AP/Wide World Photos*

Mourners gather outside of Graceland upon hearing of the death of Elvis on August 17, 1977.

The tragedy was compounded later in the day when an 18-year-old drunk driver careened into the crowd, killing two teenage girls and severely injuring two others.

PAGE 103   *AP/Wide World Photos*

The mass grieving was not confined to America alone. Here a fan consoles another at an Elvis Presley fan club in England.

PAGE 105   *AP/Wide World Photos*

Pallbearers carry Elvis's coffin into the church.

Following the funeral, Presley's body would be taken to Forest Hill Cemetery where he would be interned in a mausoleum. Less than a year later, amidst threats of grave robbing, Presley's body and that of his mother were moved to the grounds of Graceland.

PAGE 107   *Patrick Higgins*

Elvis's now famous grave marker. Note the mis-spelling of the name "Aaron." You may want to note the spelling of his middle name as it appears in his yearbook on page 21.

PAGE 109   *The New York Times*

PAGE 111   *Weekly World News*

PAGE 113   *Patrick Higgins*

The stone wall surrounding Graceland is covered with messages to Elvis, as well as various remembrances.

PAGE 115   *Lloyd Shearer*

PAGE 117   *Archive Photos*

Elvis listens to takes during the recording session of "Loving You."

PAGE 119   *Globe Photos*

PATRICK HIGGINS lives in New York City
and visits Graceland once a year.